I Sent God a Valentine

Printed in the U.S.A
Independently published
deniweber.me

From Nana with love:

Ryan

Riis

Micah

Lavinia

Gabe

Vlad

"Jesus replied, "'You must love the Lord your God with all your heart, all your soul, and all your mind.' This is the first and greatest commandment.

A second is equally important: 'Love your neighbor as yourself.'"

Matthew 22:37-39 NLT

I made God a valentine.

It might sound silly, but it's true.

I could not think of a better time

To tell Him "I love you."

I can't give God flowers or candy,

So I'm getting a head start

To give Him what he truly wants:

To hear "I love you" from my heart.

"And you must love the Lord your God with all
your heart, all your soul, and all your
strength."
Deuteronomy 6:4–5 NLT

I found scissors and some paper,

Some bits of lace and glue.

I made something special

Because you see,

God loves me too.

"We love each other
because he loved us first."
1 John 4:19 NLT

I made my valentine to God

with lots of love and care

It needed to be special

because He's always there!

"For the Lord your God is living among
you. He is a mighty savior.
Zephaniah 3:17a NLT

so I put lots of love inside

(and hugs and kisses, too.)

For God always takes care of me

and never leaves, it's true!

He will take delight in you with gladness. With
his love, he will calm all your fears. He will
rejoice over you with joyful songs."
Zephaniah 3:17 NLT

It's important to love others

That's what God asks us to do.

So, I kept making valentines.

I knew I wasn't through.

"This is my commandment:
Love each other in the same
way I have loved you."
John 15:12 NLT

I made one for my gramma

and for the folks next door.

I kept on making valentines

till I had valentines galore!

(That means lots and lots and lots!)

I put them in the mailbox

And sent them on their way.

I hope that they bring many smiles

When they arrive on Valentine's Day!

xoxo

I feel so nice and warm inside.

I know I've shared God's love.

I'm glad I get to share the gift

God sent from up above.

Because this is a special Day,

I made a Valentine for you!

It's a little bit of God's great love

For I know He loves you, too.

"For God so loved the world that He gave His only son that whoever believes in Him shall have eternal life."

John 3:16

Be my Valentine! (and God's, too!)

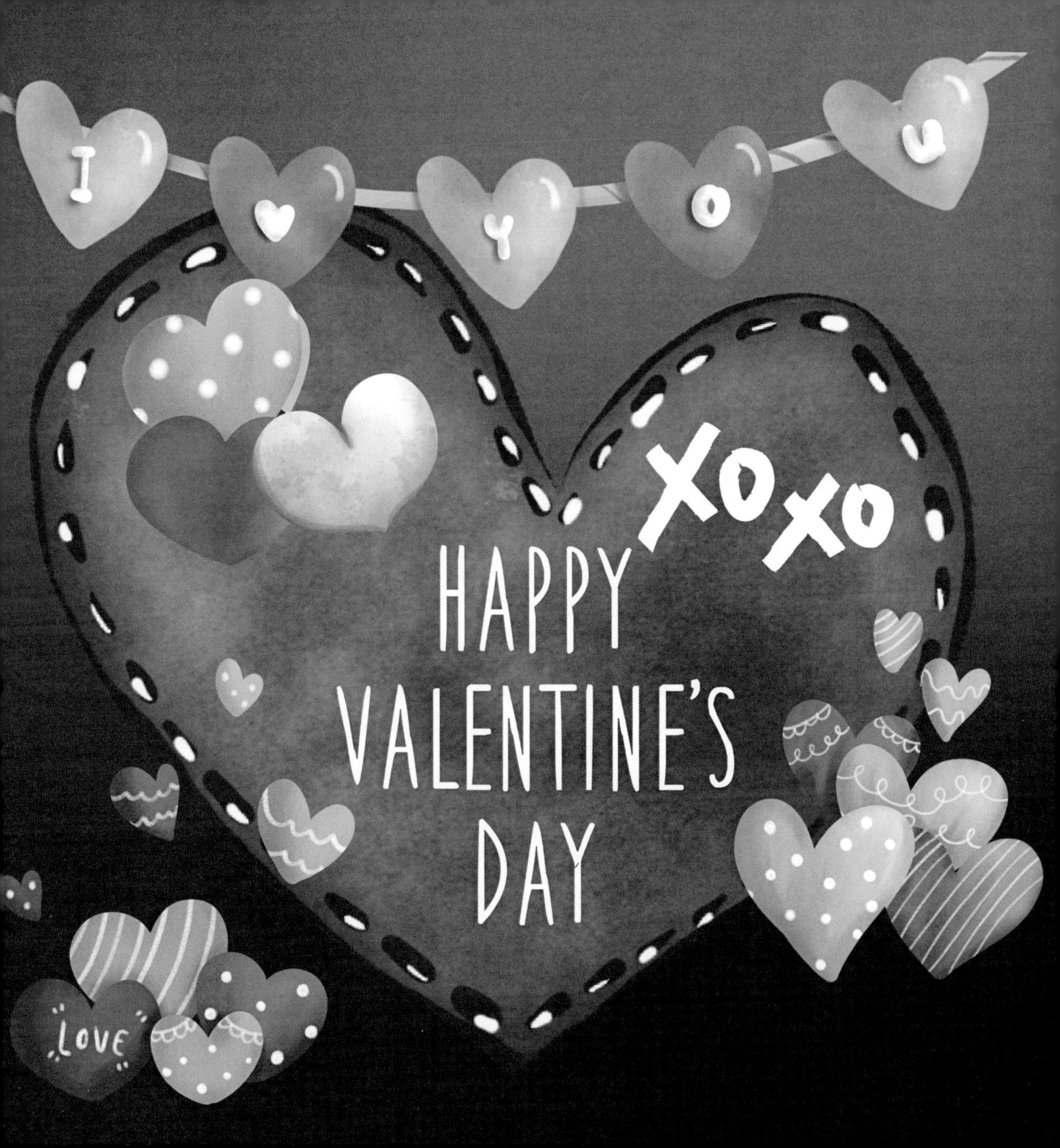
I ♥ YOU
XOXO
HAPPY VALENTINE'S DAY
LOVE

AN AVID READER SINCE THE
AGE OF FOUR , DENI
DELIGHTS IN IMAGINATIONS
AND PONDERINGS AND
HOPES TO SHARE HER LOVE
OF GOD WITH
YOUNG READERS AND
LISTENERS.

I Sent God a Valentine

is the newest addition to deni hg weber's catalog of children's books.
Her first series, "Whimsical Wonderings," takes a light-hearted
approach to stimulating curiosity and imagination in young readers.

deni enjoys reading, writing, and creating artwork in many forms. It is
her fondest hope to share the gifts God has given her with the world
around her.

XOXO

Made in the USA
Monee, IL
16 January 2024

51880113R00017